YOU  CAN

draw

brilliant

pictures

Maria Herbert-Liew

CONTENTS

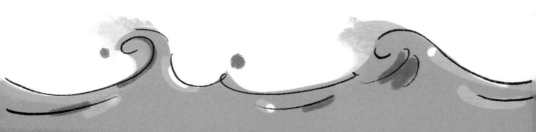

YOU CAN DRAW BRILLIANT PICTURES

Drawing is really fun! This book will give you loads of inspiration so that YOU CAN go and sketch your very own masterpieces.

Grab your pencil, turn the page, and prepare to draw some brilliant pictures! This book is full of tips, steps and ideas that you can dip into on a car journey or spend hours practising on a rainy Sunday – pictures can be drawn anywhere and anytime!

There is something for everyone – whether you want to learn to draw different people and characters, understand perspective or sketch a whole host of animals.

There is plenty of space in the book for you to practise drawing all these things, and even whole pages where you can unleash your creative side and draw entire scenes from your imagination. So what are you waiting for? Read on, and then go and draw brilliant pictures!

You might find these points helpful as you use this book.

* Look, think and draw! It's really important to use your brain and eyes every time you draw. Think about what you want to draw and look at things to help. It's a great idea to draw from real life around you, but you can also use pictures, memories, or your own imagination.

  + +

* Sketch lightly first! When you start a drawing, sketch lightly while you work out the shapes and positions. Some of the steps in this book show you the sketch lines to help you out. When you have decided where you want to draw everything then use a stronger line.

* Use your pencil as a tool! It's best to start drawing with a pencil because it is easier to control how strong you want to make your marks. Press lightly for faint marks and harder for darker marks. You can also experiment with pens and other tools. If you don't like seeing the early steps in your final drawing, you could finish with a pen and rub out the pencil marks underneath, or practise a few times on a different piece of paper first.

Now turn the page and start drawing brilliant pictures!

LINES, CURVES AND SHAPES

All drawings are made of lines, curves and shapes. Learn to see them and it will really help you to draw anything!

LINES

CURVES

SHAPES

Can you see the shapes?

Practise drawing lines,
curves and shapes here.

TIP!

Warm up!
Before drawing
anything, it's a good
idea to warm up by
practising like this.

7

ICE CREAM

Let's start with ice cream! What shapes and lines do you think we'll need?

1

Draw lines to make the bottom of the cone.

2

Lightly draw a circle on top.

3

Two scoops? Why not! Add another circle on top of the first.

4

Now draw the scoops fully, following the shapes of the circles.

5

Draw a pattern on the cone.

TIP! Add wavy lines to show how they squash down.

6 And add some toppings! You could draw wavy lines for sauce dripping down, a stick of chocolate, or tiny shapes for sweets and nuts.

Draw yours here!

BICYCLE

Looks tricky, but break it down into lines and shapes, take it one step at a time, and you can draw a bike!

1  Start with two wheels.

2 Add a small circle for the pedals near the back wheel.

3  Then draw in some pedals.

4 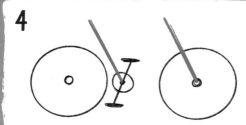 Now start the frame.

Draw two lines, one for the handlebar and one for the saddle.

5

Connect the rest of the frame.

6

Add a saddle and handlebars, and you're done! If you want, add details like a chain and spokes. You could also add some lines around the wheels to show movement.

And... Go! Draw your own bicycle here.

BUILDINGS

Drawing buildings can be easy if you start with shapes. What type of building do you want to draw?

Decide on the shape of your building.

 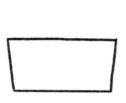 

Then add...

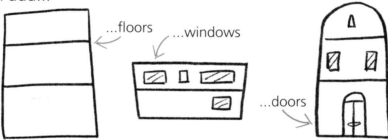

...floors   ...windows   ...doors

If you want to make it 3D, draw the side of the building.

TIP! Imagine the same shape smaller and further away. Then join it up with diagonal lines.

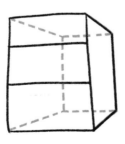

Add details and shadow too.

Have a go at drawing buildings here.

More on adding details next...

MORE ON BUILDINGS

Add details to make your buildings look real!

WINDOWS
What shape could they be?

ROOFS

Pointy? Domed? Tiled?

CHIMNEYS AND AERIALS

ARCHES

STEPS

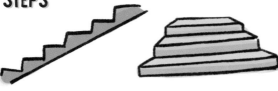

WEATHER

How about adding some weather?

Draw a building with some details here.

PEOPLE

Drawing people can be quite hard! Keep practising and you'll get better and better.

1

Lightly draw a circle for a head.

2

Then add a neck, body and arms.

3

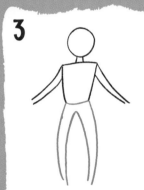

Next, add legs.

4

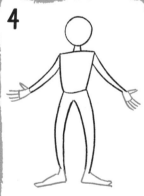

Draw in some hands and feet.

5

And to finish, add features and clothes to bring your figure to LIFE!

Practise here!

TIP! How to draw hands:

fingers will go here

basic hand shape

fingers

thumb

wrist

FACES

How about faces? Here are some tips that might help.

1 Draw a round shape for a head.

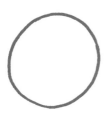

2 Add eyes and ears.

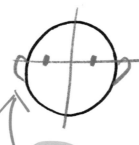

3 Then a nose and mouth.

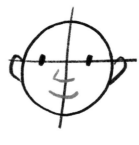

TIP! Eyes are at the same height as ears. You can use a cross to help.

4 Add some hair…

…and you're done!

Draw some faces of your own here.

TIP! Child: draw bigger eyes lower down, and a smaller nose and ears.

Adult: draw smaller eyes higher up, and a bigger nose and ears.

MORE ON FACES

How is your person feeling? Here are some tips on drawing emotions.

TIP! Use a mirror! Make some different expressions and watch how your face changes. Now try and draw it!

HAPPY

Big smiles, eyes are sometimes squeezed tight and there may be dimples.

Exaggerate and draw everything with emotion – even hair!

SAD

Everything droops down when we feel sad. Think about using the eyebrows as well as the mouth.

SURPRISED

Mouths and eyes wide open. Raised eyebrows are probably the most important part to remember!

ANGRY

Quite tricky – a good one to try out in the mirror! Head usually tilts forwards, and you can draw scrunched-up shoulders too.

A snarling mouth and eyebrows pointing down.

Practise drawing some expressions here.

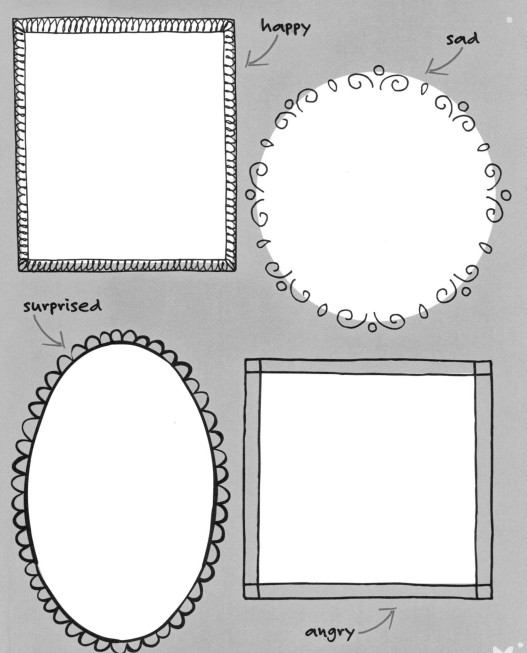

happy

sad

surprised

angry

CHARACTERS – CLOTHES

What else do you think adds character to people? How about clothes?

QUEEN

Crown (with lots of precious jewels)

Robe (to show how important and powerful she is)

Pretty decorated gown

SUPERHERO

Mask (to hide true identity)

Cape (flying around in the wind)

Boots (for grip when running fast)

COWBOY

Lasso (to herd cattle)

Hat (to shade the head from the sun)

Boots (for tough weather and long rides)

Draw your own character here.
What are they wearing?

CHARACTERS – MOVEMENT

If you really want to bring your characters to life, you can use movement.

FLYING

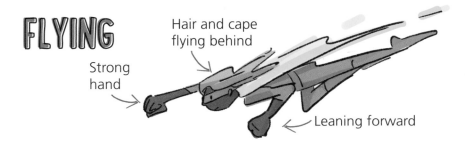

Hair and cape flying behind

Strong hand

Leaning forward

CELEBRATING

Crown jumping off the head

Hands open and out

Feet leaping off the ground

MOPING

Head bowed

Shoulders hunched

Feet and rope dragging on the ground

Practise drawing a character with movement. How do they feel? Why are they moving like that?

DRAW YOUR OWN CHARACTERS

Here's some more space to draw characters.
Who are they and what are they doing?
Try and describe this by drawing
expressions, clothes and movement.

PLANTS

1 Draw a pot (or whatever the plant is growing out of).

2 Add some stems for flowers and leaves.

TIP! Plants usually grow up and outwards.

3 Draw leaves.

4 Add flowers and you're done!

Draw a plant of your own
on the window ledge below.

More tips on drawing flowers and leaves next...

FLOWERS AND LEAVES

Flowers can have many petals...

...or just a few.

Flowers can be small...

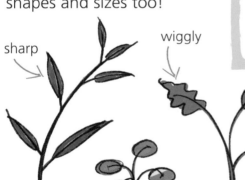

...or big.

You can draw them facing the front, side or back.

Leaves can be all sorts of shapes and sizes too!

sharp

wiggly

droopy

spiky

round

They can be colourful...

...or patterned.

Practise drawing leaves and flowers here.

INSECTS

Let's draw some insects!
What do they have in common?

Start with the head. Add eyes and antennae. ⇨ Then draw in the body. They can be long, round or thin – you'll see all shapes and sizes. ⇨ Finally, add legs (6) and wings (usually 2 or 4, if they have them).

ANT

  ⇨  ⇨

DRAGONFLY

  ⇨  ⇨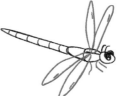

BEETLE

  ⇨  ⇨

Draw some insects here.
What shape are they? Can they fly?
Do they have long or short legs?

FRUIT & VEG

Fruit and vegetables are a great way to practise drawing at home. Go grab some now, and get drawing!

BANANA

long curves

chubby stalk

PEAR

triangle on top

circle

stalk

STRAWBERRIES

circles

triangles on bottom

stalks like flowers

tiny seeds

CARROT

thin, long cone

textured marks on skin

MUSHROOMS

round shapes

stalk can be hidden

curve where stalk comes out

Practise drawing your fruit
and vegetables here.

TIP! Don't worry
about perfect shapes
and lines. Fruit and
veg are pretty wonky
in real life!

TREES

There are lots of types of trees, and lots of ways to draw them. Look for trees outside to copy! Here are some tips to help.

Decide on the kind of shape you want your tree to be.

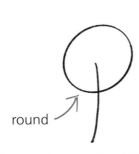

round

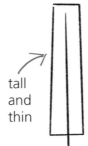

tall and thin

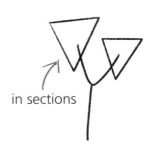

in sections

Then add a trunk, branches and leaves.

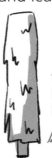

trunk hidden by leaves

no leaves

You can make them really simple.

a basic shape with swirly lines

sections of leaves as blobs

Try drawing some trees here.

MORE ON TREES

LEAVES How are the leaves growing?

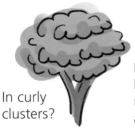

In curly clusters?

Big leaves reaching up and out?

Individual, small leaves on branches?

TRUNKS If you're drawing tree trunks in more detail, do they have a pattern? Or maybe a gnarly knot in the middle?

ROOTS What's at the bottom of the tree?

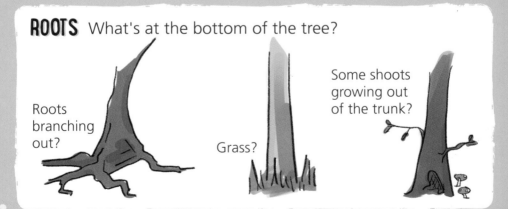

Roots branching out?

Grass?

Some shoots growing out of the trunk?

Draw some more trees, thinking about some of these things.

PERSPECTIVE

What is perspective? In drawing it means showing distance or depth. It's a tricky skill to master, but here are the basics.

HORIZON

If you're looking at a view and can see far away, you can probably see the horizon. It's where the ground stops and the sky begins, a long straight line in the distance.

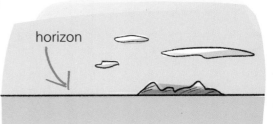

horizon

PERSPECTIVE

You can use the horizon to show perspective. The basic rule is that things nearby look big, and things far away look small. Things look smaller the closer they get to the horizon...

...until they vanish out of sight! This is called a 'vanishing point'.

TIP! The further away something is, the less detail we see. A city in the distance will just look like a lot of small shapes stuck together.

You can use a vanishing point as a guide if you want to use perspective in your drawings. Here's how:

1 Draw a line with a dot (this dot is your vanishing point).

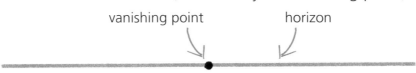

vanishing point   horizon

2 Now draw diagonal lines from that point. These lines are your guide.

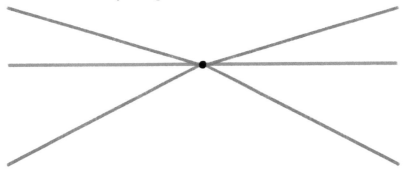

3 Draw objects along these lines, getting smaller towards the vanishing point.

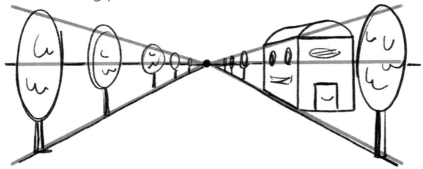

Turn the page to draw your own picture using perspective!

DRAW USING PERSPECTIVE

Now it's your turn! Follow these lines as a guide and draw a city scene using perspective. Draw buildings, trees, clouds and maybe some people. You choose!

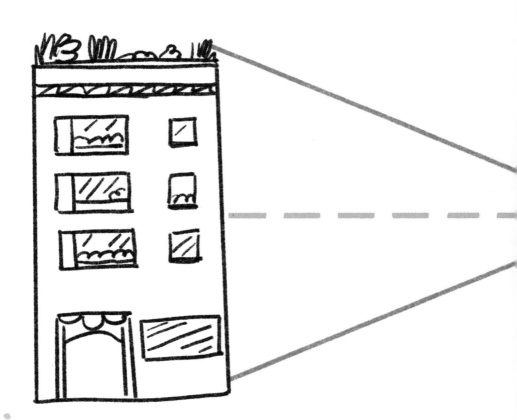

TIP!
Practise what you learnt about drawing buildings earlier, and remember to add some details.

CLOUDS

Clouds can be all sorts of shapes. Look up and notice how different they can be...

SOLID

Draw the bottoms flat with curvy lines on top. Use shadow to show they are heavy and solid.

Use criss-cross lines to draw shadow.

WISPY

Draw some wavy lines going in the same direction. Think about if there's wind blowing and which way the clouds will be moving.

PUFFY

Sometimes clouds can look like puffs or little round spots.

LONG AND THIN

Try some clouds that are long and stretched out.

IRREGULAR

Clouds can also be funny shapes. Make up your own!

Here's some space for your own clouds.

PLANE

1 Start lightly with a tick!

2 Add a line to make a cross, a third from the front of the plane. This will be where the wings sit.

3 Draw a teardrop shape for the body of the plane.

The front has a 'nose'.

4 Add the wings and tail.

5 And draw some windows and clouds.

Swoosh... we're off! Draw a plane here.

HOT AIR BALLOON

1
Lightly draw a circle.

2
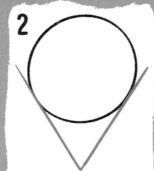

Draw two diagonal lines and join them in the middle.

3

Add an oval shape.

4

Join those shapes up to make the balloon.

5

Add a basket underneath.

6

Decorate the balloon and add some people.

Practise here!

TIP! Draw in some clouds and birds in the background to make the balloon fly! You could also add a horizon line and make the balloon smaller so it seems further away.

CASTLE

1 Start off with some basic shapes side-by-side and on top of each other.

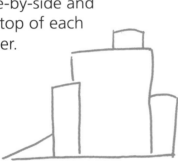

2 Turn those shapes into a building by adding floors, roofs and stairs.

3 Now add some windows and a gated entrance.

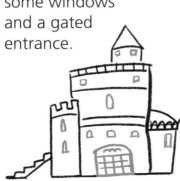

4 Add details to make it more like a castle – bricks, flags and torches.

5 And add some shadow for depth.

Draw your own castle here.

FIRE

This is the basic shape – a triangle, with an inner and outer flame.

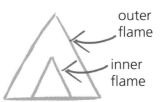

outer flame

inner flame

You can make the fire bigger by adding another section or two.

There may be wind blowing it to one side.

Draw wavy lines, following the shapes of the triangles.

To make the fire stronger, add more wavy bits going up, and some blobs coming off the flames.

Add smoke, with curls at the top.

TIP! Remember drawing clouds? Use the same techniques here for smoke.

Practise drawing fire here.

What is burning?

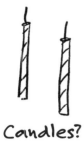

Candles?

A castle torch?

A campfire?

LANDSCAPE

Let's draw a landscape with a river and mountains. Can you remember how to use perspective?

1 Lightly sketch a horizon line and vanishing point, then add two guide lines to help you with perspective.

2 Use the guidelines to draw a river that disappears towards the vanishing point.

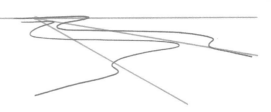

3 Draw some mountains – you can use triangles as a guide.

4 Add more
mountains
further away
and closer to
the horizon.

5 Now some
detail – how
about snow?
And animals
and trees?

Draw a landscape here.

TIP! Just remember that 'things
that are far away look
smaller' and your drawings
will have some perspective.

BIRD

1 Lightly draw a round shape and an oval shape for the head and body.

2 To help you find a bird shape, add a triangle.

3 Now draw the eye, beak and head.

Birds' eyes are quite big.

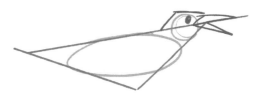

4 Draw in the rest of the body, using the round and oval shapes, and triangle, as a guide.

5 Add feathers.

6 And legs.

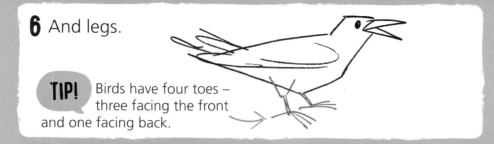

TIP! Birds have four toes – three facing the front and one facing back.

Ca-caw! Now you try!

MONKEY

1 Start with a light sketch.

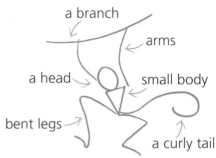

a branch

arms

a head

small body

bent legs

a curly tail

2 Then draw hairy, long arms.

3 Add a head with ears sticking out.

TIP! The lower half of the face sticks out so make it smaller than the top half.

4 Now draw a small body...

5 ...a tail, long, hairy legs and feet.

Monkeys' feet look like hands.

Draw
a monkey
swinging
from this
branch!

CROCODILE

1 Start by lightly sketching in a triangular head, a long spine and tail, and legs.

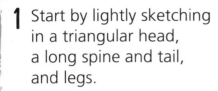

2 Draw in the head.

pointy snout

high eye sockets

sharp, jagged teeth

3 Draw the back using wiggly lines.

4 Now draw in the rest of the body and short, chubby legs.

The front legs curve forwards...

...the back legs curve backwards.

Your turn!
Draw a croc next to the pond.

TIP! Add some more texture to the skin when you've finished – a criss-cross pattern looks good!

ELEPHANT

There are lots of shapes and lines that make up an elephant.

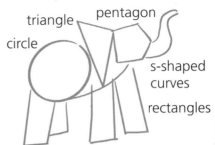

triangle

pentagon

circle

s-shaped curves

rectangles

1 Start by drawing a big ear and a small eye.

2 Then add the head and curvy trunk.

3 Draw strong, thick legs, the body and tail.

4 Finally, draw a tusk, and some wrinkles and folds.

Have a go at drawing an elephant here.

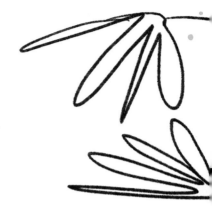

SNAKE

1 Lightly draw an oval for a head, and a twisty line for where the body will go.

2 Now draw the head – a hexagon shape with a flat top and pointy chin. The mouth is a wide curve joining up the sides.

3 Using the twisty line as your guide, draw the body. End with a pointy tail.

4 Draw the face – big eyes, small nostrils and a long, forked tongue.

Some snakes have slit pupils instead of round ones.

5 Add some pattern, keeping it on the top side of the body.

Draw some motion lines too!

Your turn! Draw a snake here.

RAINFOREST

What kinds of things do you
think live in a rainforest?
Here are some ideas.

wiggly, trailing vines

a waterfall

butterflies
and
unusual
bugs

very tall
trees

thick,
dark tree
trunks in
the shade

big leaves

flowers
and more
big leaves

a green forest floor

Draw some of these things here, then turn the page to create your own rainforest.

DRAW A RAINFOREST

Use this space to draw your own rainforest.

TIP! Rainforests are wet places, and can be quite dark and shady. Try adding shadows and patches of light to make it come alive!

Don't forget to add
some creatures!
How about
some birds,
reptiles or monkeys?
And an explorer?

THE SEA

Now let's draw the sea! What kind of sea do you want to draw?

CALM

A calm sea will be very flat and steady, just a few horizontal lines to show moving water.

ROUGH

A rough sea will have lots of messy, wavy lines, some high and some low.

TIP! If you're using colour, leave some white parts to show light reflecting off the water.

Draw a stormy sea in the space below.

Waves will always travel in one direction. They roll up, then back down again.

up

down

travelling in this directon

Even if the waves are really wild and irregular, they will still travel in the same direction.

TIP! You can add shadow under some of the waves to show how big and heavy they are.

BOAT

1 Draw a rectangular shape with diagonal sides going downwards. The top is longer than the bottom.

2 Next, draw a cross for a mast, with the horizontal line the same direction as the top of the boat.

3 Now add the sails! Add triangles to the mast – they can be straight or curved, depending on if the wind is blowing.

4 Put some details in to make your boat look real!

Don't forget the sea!

Draw your own boat on these waves.

POLAR BEAR

1 Lightly sketch out the shape of the bear – a big triangle with legs.

2 Start by drawing the head.

small ear

pointy with a black nose

3 Draw in the front leg. The legs are really big.

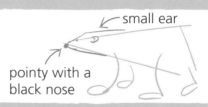

4 Then the rest of the body.

polar bears have big bottoms

5 Draw in the other legs.

6 Add some small dashes to make the bear look furry, and finish with some claws.

Draw your polar bear here.

OCTOPUS

1 Draw the body to start. Then lightly draw in 8 twisty lines (for the tentacles).

2 On the head, add some eyes with a wavy line on top.

3 Start to draw in the tentacles. They join together with a curve, a bit like an 'H'.

4 Finish the tentacles with twisty, wiggly shapes (like snakes).

TIP!

Look between your fingers and toes – octopus tentacles join up in the same way!

5 Now do the rest!

6 Add some suckers under the tentacles to finish.

Draw an octopus here.

FISH

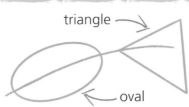

triangle

oval

1 Imagine a line running through the fish. Lightly draw the basic shapes to start.

2 Draw a body and tail using curved lines.

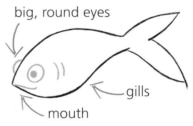

big, round eyes

gills

mouth

3 Add features.

4 Then add fins.

5 Draw some pattern onto the fins, and scales on the body.

Now have a go at
drawing your own fish
in this fish bowl.

CRAB

1 Start with a curve.

Then add a wavy line for the top half of the crab.

2 Finish the body with another curved line.

And add a face!

3 Draw eight back legs.

TIP! The legs bend sharply and are in segments. They have pointy ends.

4 Add two front legs with big claws to finish.

This is a tricky one! Take it slowly and practise here.

MERMAID

Mermaids are mythical creatures, half human and half fish. Can you imagine how they would look?

1 Lightly sketch a head, chest and arms, then a long line from head to tail.

2 Draw in a face and add some wavy lines for hair.

3 Now draw the arms, hands and chest.

4 Then add a tail with a fin.

5 Fill in the hair and add some patterns to finish.

Draw a mermaid of your own here.

SHARK

1 Start with a teardrop shape.

2 Draw a tail fin.

3 Then add a big top fin and two underneath.

4 Now draw these important parts.

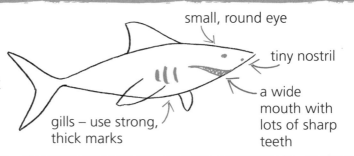

small, round eye

tiny nostril

a wide mouth with lots of sharp teeth

gills – use strong, thick marks

Draw a shark here.

DRAW AN UNDERWATER SCENE

Here's some space for you to draw your own underwater scene. Draw what you think is happening underneath the waves!

ROCKET

Let's go into space! Here's how to draw a rocket. Build it up section by section.

Start at the tip. This one has a thin line at the very top.

Add on the next section.

TIP! Think about the shapes you might use. Can you see rectangles, triangles, cylinders?

Draw the main body.

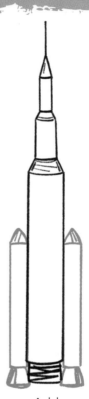

Add some rocket boosters.

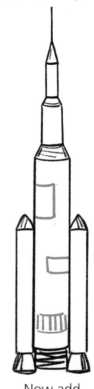

Now add some details on the main body to finish.

...And lift off! Practise drawing a rocket here. You could make yours with different shapes and sections.

Don't forget to add a blast of fuel too!

SPACE

What might you find in space?

satellite

moon

stars

astronaut

planets

rover

Draw some things in space here.

ALIEN

How about aliens? Copy this one or make up your own!

1 What does it look like?

2 Does it walk? Slide? Swim?

3 Does it have arms? Tentacles? Wings?

4 How does it communicate?

Draw an alien here.

DRAW SOMEWHERE IN OUTER SPACE

Imagine somewhere in outer space and draw it here. Think about buildings, vehicles, characters, plants and maybe even alien food!

TIP! Remember all the things you've learnt in this book, and try drawing something completely new!

What's here?

Here's a...?

And this?

Here?

Goodbye, have fun!

Published by Collins
An imprint of HarperCollins Publishers
Westerhill Road, Bishopbriggs, Glasgow, G64 2QT

HarperCollins Publishers
1st Floor, Watermarque Building, Ringsend Road, Dublin 4, Ireland

www.harpercollins.co.uk

Publisher: Michelle I'Anson
Project manager: Rachel Allegro
Cover: Kevin Robbins

9780008372668

Printed in Bosnia and Herzegovina

10 9 8 7 6 5 4 3 2